The Zen of La Llorona

DEBORAH A. MIRANDA is of Esselen, Chumash, French and Jewish ancestry. She is enrolled with the Ohlone-Costanoan Esselen Nation of California. Her collection *Indian Cartography* won the Diane Decorah First Book Award. Her poetry is widely published in such anthologies as *The Dirt is Red Here: Art and Poetry from Native California* (HeyDay Books, 2002) and *The Eye of the Deer: An Anthology of Native American Women Writers* (Aunt Lute, 1999). Currently, Deborah is Assistant Professor of English at Washington and Lee University, where she teaches Creative Writing, Composition, and Native American Literatures.

Earthworks Series
Series Editor: Janet McAdams

HEID E. ERDRICH: *The Mother's Tongue*
DIANE GLANCY: *Rooms: New and Selected Poems*
LEANNE HOWE: *Evidence of Red: Poems and Prose*
DEBORAH A. MIRANDA: *The Zen of La Llorona*
CARTER REVARD: *How the Songs Come Down: New and Selected Poems*

The Zen of La Llorona

DEBORAH A. MIRANDA

CAMBRIDGE

PUBLISHED BY SALT PUBLISHING
PO Box 937, Great Wilbraham, Cambridge PDO CB1 5JX United Kingdom

© Deborah Miranda, 2005

The right of Deborah Miranda to be identified as the
author of this work has been asserted by her in accordance
with Section 77 of the Copyright, Designs and Patents Act 1988.

First published 2005

Printed and bound in the United Kingdom by Lightning Source

Typeset in Swift 9.5 / 13

ISBN 1 84471 063 7 paperback

.

SP

1 3 5 7 9 8 6 4 2

for Margo

Contents

The Legend(s) of the Weeping Woman   1

PART ONE: PASSAGE   5
Passage   7
Three Months Without Electricity   8
Petroglyph   9
Deer   10
Sisters in Rain   11
Jenny   12
Almost a Pantoum for My Mother   13
After San Quentin   14
Last Confession   18
The Zen of La Llorona   20
Our Lady of Perpetual Loss   21
November Leaves   22
Forty   23
I'm Lost   28
April Sixteenth   29
Swarm   31
Things My Mother Taught Me   32
Advice from La Llorona   33
First Step   34

PART TWO: DROWNING   37
Drowning   39
Tongues   40
Duende   41
Echolocation   42
La Llorona's Daughter   43
Sleeping Beauty, 1978   45

Chianti	46
The Twin Sister Your Mother Never Mentioned	47
The Place Where Grief and Rage Live	48
Husband	51
10%	52
Driving Past Suicide for Three Novembers	54
Separation	55
Ex	56
The Language of Prophets	57
Heron	58
PART THREE: A TRICK OF GRACE	59
A Trick of Grace	61
Arrow Song	63
From a Dream, I Wake to Tender Music	64
Love Poem to a Butch Woman	65
Mesa Verde	66
Music Like Red Earth	67
First Time	69
Steele Street	70
A Ceremony for Giving You Up	72
Clean	73
Shopping	74
Old Territory. New Maps.	75
Dawn	78
Burning the Baskets (triptych)	81
PART FOUR: DAR A LUZ	85
Dar a Luz	87
Portrait of the Beloved as a Young Lifeguard	88
Smoke	90
My Moon	92

Home   93
Fencing Out the Deer   94
Satiate   96
Shenandoah   97
When I Think of You   99
Leaving Oz   100
Tenderness   102
Highway 126   103
Mitzvah   105
dia de las muertas   106

Acknowledgments

Thanks to those who have supported me in this work: my *compañeras y compañeros* at the Macondo Workshop (especially Sandra Cisneros, who believes in the *duende* in us all), my colleagues at Pacific Lutheran University in Tacoma, and my new colleagues at Washington and Lee University in Lexington. Deepest thanks to those whose work inspires and sustains me: Rosalind Bell, Ahimsa Timoteo Bodhrán, Chrystos, Qwo-Li Driskill, Linda Hogan, AnaLouise Keating, Janet McAdams, Magda Nieves and Lori Anderson, Beverly Slapin. Each of you gift me with words and love, each contributes to the music that keeps my *duende* alive and dancing. May I do the same for you.

Some of these poems have been published previously, or are forthcoming, in the following journals and anthologies: *Bellowing Ark, Canterbury Faire Poets; Study of American Indian Literatures; Wilderness; The Dirt is Red Here: Contemporary Native California Poetry and Art; Bearing Witness, Reading Lives: Imagination, Creativity & Cultural Change; Through the Eye of the Deer: Contemporary Animal Poems and Stories by American Indian Women; Wild Song: Poems of the Natural World; The Bellingham Review; Weber Studies Journal* and *West Wind Review*.

The Zen of La Llorona

The Legend(s) of the Weeping Woman

For Indians, mestizos, and Chicanas of the Conquest, she is La Llorona, an Indian woman claimed by a Spaniard as part of his reward for furthering the colonization of North America. The Indian woman, whose real name may have been Maria, Marina, or even Malinche, bears beautiful children whom she loves even as they tie her more tightly to her captor. When the Spaniard betrays the Indian woman (with another woman? by going back to his 'real 'family in Spain? by attempting to steal away to Spain with the Indian children?—we cannot know, except to say that betrayal is an unfathomable wound), she is enraged and helpless beyond reason. She takes up a knife, slits the throats of her dear babies, and throws their bodies into the river.

The story goes that La Llorona becomes a ghost who haunts riverbanks and lonely places after dark, moaning, "Ai, Ai, mis hijos!" If she finds any children left alone or out by themselves, she may mistake them for her own and attempt to take them into the spirit world with her. Her grief is so powerful that she can reach out of her pain and draw others into it, where they will never escape. I agree that her grief is very real. But I think there's a still deeper loss that La Llorona knows: Only after murdering her own children does she see the Spaniard's true victory. He has stolen more than her land, her body, her children. He has stolen her power to create; he has transformed her into a destroyer like himself.

Human cultures around the world know this woman all too well. La Llorona is the name that I know her by, but she has other names in stories from other places, of which these are only a few: Rachel, Banshee, Niobe, Medea, Mesulina, Lamia, Margaret Garner, Susan Smith. Each one of these La Llorona stories testify to an entire world out of balance, a culture in which the creative force has been driven mad, desecrated itself and its purpose. It's not surprising that the stories go back into the oral history of Europe, or that they continue to this day. The stories are lessons about self-betrayal and grief: Be vigilant, maintain an active and sincere relationship with power, with the powers of the earth, our minds, bodies, hearts, and the hearts of others.

My grandmother, Marquesa, told my father and his brothers the story of La Llorona in a walnut orchard late one night, as they huddled in their tent after picking all day, and heard a weird, horrific wail out among the trees. Much later my maternal grandmother, Doris, told me the story of how my mother married too young, lost a baby to neglect and a man's rage, grieved all the rest of her life in destruction and despair—and took her remaining children along with her through hell. I grew up with the cries of La Llorona in my ears every night, every day. I fattened on those tears: my lullaby, my drink, the air I breathed. Fear and anger, depression and self-loathing lurked in my blood all year, surfaced on marked and unmarked anniversaries, possessed me. As I grew older, triggered by events in my own life that I could never foresee, I came perilously close to bearing La Llorona's grief myself, perpetuating that power gone insane. La Llorona is not a legend I can tell my own children, and then put back on the shelf, encased within paper and binding.

I am La Llorona's daughter. I should have drowned, but I didn't. Something old, strong, and tender cradled me in that river, taught me how to swim. My own blood drew me out of that river, took me home, dried me off. Yes, I'm a terrible swimmer. I can't see without my glasses, don't know how to regulate my breath, don't trust myself to a rhythm that will keep me afloat. But somehow, I swim. And I've learned that, just as La Virgen de Guadalupe emerges from the sacred ruins of the older indigenous goddess Tonantzin, La Llorona emerges from the ancient deity Cihuacoatl—originally the patron of midwives, who helped women bear healthy children, and sanctified women who died in child-birth. Significantly, Cihuacoatl knows both creation, and death — the full story — not just grief but also the crucial counterpoint of joy. First by the militaristic Aztec-Mexicas, and then by the colonizing Spaniards, Cihuacoatl's creative powers were de-emphasized, and her destructive qualities heavily privileged. Cihuacoatl was made, quite literally, unbalanced—turned into a half-person, incapable of a whole and healthy identity. Thus was La Llorona constituted, a woman capable only of worshipping loss; passing on that twisted religion of devastation to her children and every dwindling generation that follows.

Love and the erotic are powerfully creative forces in human lives, in what Joy Harjo calls, 'The epic search for grace"—grace being another word for a self-sustaining matrix, a wholeness, the act of living as a balanced being within a balanced world. Grace isn't about a culminating moment of perfection or the achievement of a sublime mystical state. Grace, or what I call an indigenous erotic, has a particular context for this particular continent: the perpetual act of balancing—always working toward balance through one's actions, intent, and understanding of the world. But both love and the erotic are at odds with the violence and domination that structures any colonizing or patriarchal culture. Thus, in colonization and patriarchy love is turned into grief, and the erotic is distorted into the pornographic oppression and exploitation of the bodies of women and children, and thus eventually, men. These oppressors are anyone seeking power in a patriarchal system—men *and* women — and the system, once the creative/erotic element is betrayed, perpetuates itself. For me, life began again when I gave birth to my own children. I tasted creation: discovered an ability to love and appreciate that I'd never experienced. Having children graced me with the gift, however fleeting and embattled, of utter tenderness and love. That was when I began to recover from my own drowning. I could fight harder for myself—love myself, unlearn destruction—when my survival also nurtured my children's lives. But it is the curiously twinned stories of my indigenous California people, and my mother's inconsolable grief, that allow me to ride out a devastating current.

And why does any of this matter to anyone but myself? At this point in global history, we are *all* La Llorona's children. We are all howling, mourning, grieving for losses that seem unbearable. The old stories show us how we were betrayed, how we betrayed ourselves and our own powers of creation. We must know those stories as starting places, not

[3]

endings. We must teach our children how to embrace all the aspects of the creative, and *live*. For me, this means learning to ask myself questions I'd never imagined before:

What if La Llorona's daughter *survived*?

What if this daughter born of destroyers met with love?

How could such a child possibly know how to honor that gift?

I ask these questions because they are central to our lives as human beings, and to mine as a daughter, a mother, and as a lover. These poems are a record of my journey out of destruction and into a North American indigenous state of creativity, the erotic, and joy. These poems exist because my ancestors survived, and we swim out of a river of betrayal — those girls, women, boys, men, and elders—and maintain a thread of memory, a knowledge of grace, that teaches and guides us even now.

This book is for all of those ancestors known and unknown, named and unnamed; for my children, for my mother, for my brothers and sisters, and especially for my lover and companion, Margo.

DEBORAH MIRANDA
September 2004
Lexington, Virginia

Part One: *Passage*

Passage

Red and gold wash my study at dawn,
light seeping through fine lace curtains.
I imagine this is the same glow
my wide-open fetal eyes craved,
seeking candent mysteries
behind the wall of my mother's belly.

She walked carefully in the days of her final
pregnancy knowing, like Sarah, she was blessed;
a child of impossible conception rolling
within her body as naturally as ships
ride the swells of foreign seas.
Sarah laughed at such miracles,
but her audacity did not occur to my mother
—laughter might have dislodged
what doctors warned was precarious moorage.

So I floated, more and more snugly,
absorbed L.A. sun, swish of cars on freeway,
shade under gracious palms; my mother's voice
a powerful surge of sound translated through the mist
of heartbeats, arteries rushing, bowels
groaning under my ripening form:

this way, this way! Until I found the current,
shot down the passage into morning,
the clear song of my mother's cries
naming me *Deborah, Deborah.*

Three Months Without Electricity

She lets me hold the porcelain shell.
My fingers glow warm apricot;
illuminated cup of blood and bone.
Mama balances a tray of flame,
brilliant gold igniting the edges of her body.
In our tiny bathroom, she sets candles
at each corner of the small tub,
around the vanity, back of the toilet.
Small pearls of light shoot up the pink tiles
and onto the shadowed ceiling.
Heat waves undulate along the lower parts of walls.
In the warm water, I am first a fish,
then a dark seal, then a turtle, peering out of my ocean
to see the wax well up, lucid, drench
the burning air of my mother's silence

Petroglyph

Snow falls that night,
spreads heavy and smooth
like stone, like white granite.
It takes the sharp cut of deer tracks.

In nightgown and bare feet,
she follows a string
of cloven hearts wandering from the woods,
past the barn with its scents of straw,

cats, cobwebs; lapping the length
of the skinny tin trailer
where the girl had lain curled
in dreams of slow words; past

her father's red truck
asleep in the driveway, dents filling with snow,
tools covered in the bed made
fresh and clean, no trace

of labor, his sweat, jumbled scraps of lumber; down
the long driveway, to enter mute pines
and bare maples at the mouth of the road
that leads away.

She stands breathing in silvered swirls, heart
thumping; *this is as far as I go*. Snow
takes her print, curved half-moons
cut by the heat of childhood in skin.

Deer

They hang her in the barn, head down, tongue fat,
dripping blood. I am left alone
for a moment, venture close to stroke dark fur
made rough by winter; that is when she is whole,
intact before butchering. I'm not sure
if they shot her, or hit her by accident
with the truck, but she comes from the mountains
out if season so it is the darkness that counts, not
how she died. All winter long we'll eat her
in secret: steaks, stews, bones boiled for broth
and the dogs. But what I will remember is
the rough way men's hands turn back the hide, jerk
down hard to tear it from her body. A dull hunting
knife cracks and disjoints the carcass.
Dismembers it piece by piece.
The hide disappears—left untanned, taken
to the dump. Years afterward I walk
out to the barn, scrape my foot against
the stained floor beneath the crossbeam,
never tell anyone
                    I've been taken like that.

Sisters in Rain

Too close to the school
to be bussed, too broke
to own cars, too cool to carry
umbrellas, we walk
every day, every winter, three years
of wet shoes, jeans tight
around cold knees, slick rivers
of copper, black, chestnut, gold, chocolate
flowing down our backs. We boast
of strength, silkiness, mysterious power
given by rain's cleansing.

At the end of the day we meet to strip,
wring wool sweaters, let them steam on damp towels
to the rhythm of brass buttons in the dryer.
Five girls in bras and panties
we comb out each other's pride, strand
by strand, against luminous skin
in a world without fathers, brothers, mates.
We must be each other's mothers, aunts, grandmothers:
sisters, all there is,
all we count on to last.

Jenny

Copper curls, slow blue eyes,
    alone.
She waits for my patient good will.
    I flare
white-hot like the heart of a mountain,
    sudden:
The old anger of my childhood.
    I've lived
knowing the truth, not wanting it.
    Abandonment
happens; do I think it goes
    away
because safety houses me now?
    Do I fear
her lostness is contagious, like lice,
    little bits
leaping off her thin, crooked body?
    Child, move on.
You upset my web, the fabricated home
    of my memories.

Almost a Pantoum for My Mother

She spoke rarely, and quietly. We walked to the bus stop,
wind blew in our faces, water dripped from our hair.
The trailer court's sooty asphalt swam in oily rainbows.
It was my mother's first winter. We held on the best we could,

wind blew in our faces, water dripped from our hair.
Now, with my own child, I am a small spinning universe
far from my mother's first winter. She held on the best she could
barely tethered by our living link of arm, hand, fingers.

Now, my own child is a small spinning universe
holds my hand while the best part of me slips away,
barely tethered by our living link of arm, hand, fingers.
Did my mother feel this too, beneath clouds heavy as clay?

I hold my daughter's hand, the best part of me echoing footsteps
I rarely speak quietly. We walk to the bus stop
beneath clouds heavy as clay, as potholes
in sooty asphalt, swimming in rainbows.

We hold on the best we can.

After San Quentin
for my father, who asks why

I

We are his inmates, the trailer
our prison.
It's all here: riots, accusations,
the leather strap of justice rising and falling.
On his belt my father carries
keys to the front door, his truck,
our hearts swinging
like scalps.

He's forgotten what walls are for,
how doors function—honorable shuttings,
framed sweep of opening—
so long in a place
where each movement he made is chronicled,
my father became like them:
suspicious, a watcher, slave to obsession.

II

Snapshots:
cholo grace in L.A.,
Tu Solo Tu, cigarette burning
between my mother's pale fingers.
My father's shoulder a black and white blur.
Arms circled, he holds her tightly.

Here, in pressed khakis, solemn girl
on his knee, wide wet sands—*Santa Monica;*
when I was a little boy, mi'ija, I'd swim
from pier to pier, way out to the ocean.
My mother thought I would drown.
But I didn't need air, mi'ija, I swear:
I could breathe underwater.
I wish I could remember how.

III

My father sleeps inside the bone walls
of mission and mythology,
condemned to hell slammed, bolted—
confined at night, listening,
while women and girls choke
in airless *monjeras*
suffer violations by *soldados y padres*,
like the names they force
on us, patronymics of shame.
San Quentin was not his first prison.

We don't know our own name:
generations answer to *Miranda*.
In Spain, it used to mean *looking*.
Here, Miranda means *you have the right
to remain silent . . .*
it means
our own words can and will
be used against us; it means
a court of law is not surprised
to find my father, again and again, within its gates:
and his son after him.

IV

You find a dusty shovel in the barn,
strip to your waist, heave chunks
of fallow earth. You sort out stones,
give soil air to breathe, smooth rows
tempting as cotton sheets.
Barefoot in the grateful dirt, you observe
where sun falls longest, listen
to wind through pines,
calculate slope and drainage.
You dig holes, drop life in, pull a blanket of earth
behind you with a wide foot: sweet corn,
peas, cucumbers, squash,
broccoli, garlic, green beans, tomatoes.
You stand of a warm August evening,
green hose in hand, watering.

This piece of earth is the one place
you don't fight with walls;
the only peace handed down to you.
All this time, I thought we had nothing
—no land, no prayers, no language.
I was wrong.
We are the containers
that hold our colonized history.
I turn and stir the past
for my hungry soil.
Daddy, I take your tools,
mix fury with words
down where the next generation sleeps.
Watch now as I raise nasturtiums and tomatoes,
green corn silk streaming
like Santa Ynez waters set free.

Last Confession

Emerging from deep underground caves
where his battalion took sanctuary,
my father saw the sun again,
felt his arms and legs still attached
to his body,
thought maybe
the priests were right.
Scared sacred,
he confessed everything,
was awarded
the navy-issue wafer
of forgiveness.

Now it's a hospital
in Western Washington,
my father's hair is white,
the priest gives him
a brief prayer to recite—
some little piece of magic.
Miraculously
this man forgives my father
fifty years
of drinking, adultery,
lying, violence, divorce,
abandonment,
taking the Lord's name in vain
in two languages.
My father takes
the wafer
of the Holy Catholic Church
into his mouth,
lies back on pillows:
whole again, safe.

I am a jealous daughter.
I want to be the one
who forgives my father
everything.
I want to know
where the sins go—
the ones the priest forgave.
Does he collect them
like beads on his rosary,
selecting the hardest,
brightest transgressions for God?

The Zen of La Llorona

> I have lost my favorite teacup. I have two
> choices. I can have lost my teacup and be
> miserable. I can have lost my teacup and be all
> right. In either case, the teacup is gone.
>
> — *by* CHERI HUBER

La Llorona rises over my town—
a solitary curve, sharpened by someone else's fury.

I read a small gray Zen book.
Everyone loses everything.

Lovers, families, friends, possessions, egos—
we keep nothing of this world, not even our bodies.

It's as if you'd lost your favorite teacup, you see.
No amount of searching, weeping or wailing

will bring it back. If you want a drink,
use a different container.

Write a long series of passionate poems about your cup.
Hell, write a whole book. Obsession is the mother of creation.

But as you compose, sip from the new mug.
It will become your mug of choice.

You'll lose that one, too. And so on.
In theory, anyway, we outlast dispossession:

Ceramic mugs, hearts, continents.
Outside, La Llorona's knife slices the indigo heart

of silence. *Nonsense*, she howls. *There's always
something left to lose.*

Our Lady of Perpetual Loss

Maybe all losses before this one are practice:
maybe all grief that comes after her death seems tame.
I wish I knew how to make dying simple,
wish our mother's last week were not constructed
of clear plastic tubing, IVs, oxygen hiss,
cough medicine, morphine patches, radiation tattoos,
the useless burn on her chest.
I'm still the incurable optimist, she whispers,
you're still the eternal pessimist.
My sister sleeps on a sofa; our brother, exhausted,
rolls up in a blanket on the hard floor.
Curled in a rented white bed, our mother's body
races to catch up with her driven, nomadic soul.
Those nights alone, foster care, empty beer bottles
taught us she was always already vanishing.

November Leaves

As evening descends, my daughter and her best friend rake,
wrapped in heavy coats, hats, and gloves. They scrape

the sidewalk clear of magnolia and cherry, breath coming
in heated, moist questions. Miranda puts her back into it,

heaves wet, slimy heaps into barrels. I stay inside, between
the bedroom and porch, in unbearable cusp.

Clear and safe again, the girls stand beside the steps,
rakes still, awkward soldiers at attention.

Has either girl ever seen a dead person?
The men from the mortuary carry my mother's body

down the stairs and roll the stretcher across the fine
clean sidewalk, under the plum tree's bare branches.

Wet fragments catch on muddy wheels, sticking all the way,
maybe, to distant cold storage. The girls watch,

gripping wooden handles, sweating beneath
all those layers. As the van pulls away, Epiphany

tugs off a wet glove, rests her hand
on my daughter's broad shoulder.

Forty

I.

In stories I've heard,
you flirt with extinction as if grief
were a prize you must win.
Your own birth takes three days
of dry labor, fat tumors vying
with your small body
for passage into the world. Your beginning
ends in a desperate c-section,
nearly kills your mother.

Pregnancy, a bad marriage at seventeen.
The house is full of your husband's rage
but you drink and fight as equals.
One night he locks you in the bedroom,
leaves you to sleep it off. Two toddlers
roam the house alone,
raid the medicine cabinet.
St. Joseph's Aspirin,
economy size. The loss of a child
is the sin you won't resolve:
not in divorce
not in heroin
not in this lifetime.

My conception
saves your life.
Examining your cervix
for the tell-tale signs of pregnancy,
the doctor finds cancer.
Abort the fetus,
he instructs, *plan on surgery*.

Your refusal saves my life.
Together, we survive
forty more years.

II.

Records are missing for the year you run:
my father sent to San Quentin,
two kids in foster care, me with godparents.
It's the lost year.
You give it to me
like a communicable disease.
Neither one of us ever recovers.

A blur of drunk driving in your forties.
I watch the white line
from the window on my side of the car,
call out warnings when you waver
too wildly.
I am always waiting
for you to disappear.
Is that cough another bout of pneumonia?
Do your eyes glitter with tears, or beer?
Will you get out of bed? Go to work?
Make it home?
The murky roads at night:
a smeared windshield,
pounding rain;
words like *hydroplane* and *bald tires*.
Anniversary sobs erupting
from your gut
late in June, feral
in your worship of the ghost baby.
Like a comet, the orange tip of a Pall Mall:

rising and falling
in an unlit room
against the
white chenille spread.

At midnight I find you slumped in the tub.
You've dozed off,
hair matted against your neck,
breasts pale and veined
like the rivers of a once-sovereign land,
silver beer can
perched on the edge
of a flesh-colored toilet.

For thirty more years I dream of saving your life.

III.

Sixty-six years old.
You rest lightly on the bed
in the back room of my house:
ninety pounds of hollow bone.
The salt-and-pepper braid
I wove for you earlier
sickles a half-moon
on your bird-wing shoulder.
Your hands lie open
on a blue blanket, receiving
the prize no men, drugs, or self-hatred
could ever give you.
Your oldest addiction curled up
in your chest, devours
all that survival.
I say aloud, *That's not my mother.*

Relieved for the first time
in forty years
that nothing can hurt you—

still wondering
why I couldn't open the door,
take that burning secret from your lips,
wake you
save you
one last time.

IV.

Four months from Thanksgiving
to Spring Equinox. It snowed yesterday.
Even the planet is confused.
There are no buds on the trees;
daffodils freeze in a stunted crouch
beside my house. But still
each morning grows lighter.
The Universe is an old place;
constellations don't get lost
as easily as you might think.

Mama, you entered this world
looking for the exit,
stood just inside that door
since my birth, surviving
against your will.
What's forty years,
measured in pain?

Some mysteries are good.
Some mysteries hide like little moons

behind a belt of asteroids
or in the shadow of something greater.
And some mysteries
we can't know—
aren't ours to know.

Those years you gave me, mother:
years harder than inventing god.
I never had enough,
but I'll keep those forty years,
like a message
left behind—my textbook,
my bible, my dictionary,
my atlas. You taught me this:
no life preservers. No rescuers.
No heroes charging up on white horses
or pick-up trucks.

The next forty years
hang fire in the cradle
of my own hands.

I'm Lost

in an abrupt pile of clothes
on the floor of my mother's bathroom—
collapsed legs of blue jeans,
breathless sweater flattened, deflated.
A wrinkled topography shed
like skin
just as it fell from her body
when she shrugged off her husk that last night,
before she called me to take her to the doctor, before
she never came back to this apartment.
I wish I had the courage
to pick up those clothes
or at least
read this map
hastily scrawled on the ground.

April Sixteenth

I sing Happy Birthday to a box of ashes
centered on the old wooden table you gave me.

The rest of the day I keep you at bay,
don't make a pilgrimage to Safeway

for angel food cake, orange sherbet, Martinelli's. I wonder,
what would I have given you? You never asked for much.

Socks, a vacuum cleaner, windows washed—
you'd end up exclaiming over sandlewood-scented candles,

blank books, pretty earrings you couldn't wear
because no one remembered your skin tolerated only real gold

(I found such gifts, still in wrappers,
in the bottom drawers and top shelves of your room).

Last year I probably pissed and moaned
about having to get the kids from their dad's house, drive

to Seattle in rush hour traffic to take you out to dinner—
the Moon Temple on Wallingford, Chinese food

I didn't know was bad till my more worldly lover broke the news.
I enjoyed it, anyhow:

your pleasure in pouring orange pekoe, lifting
crispy slabs of almond chicken from iceberg lettuce, heaping

thick white plates with steaming prawns, enough for you
to take home for midnight snacks. Ahead, retirement for you;

tenure-track for me. Maybe this year
I would have given you the thick cotton socks, the vacuum cleaner.

What you'd say now:
That's life! —set your mouth, light another cigarette. Keep on.

Swarm

18 months after
your last breath
I am still learning
a language
I can't translate,
a distance
I can't measure,
a weight
I can't move.
I live with it,
endure
the glacial grind
of questions
I should have asked.
Some days your scent
feathers through my blood
like a flock of mourning doves.
Some days, splintered memories
migrate from my heart
out into every cell
of this survivor's body,
sting
like a million
frenzied bees
fleeing
the broken hive.

Things My Mother Taught Me

Wear your silver and turquoise to knead tortilla dough;
baking soda polishes rings bright again.
Four paths to payday: beans and rice, flour, Crisco.

If hamburger's sparse, cut with stale bread or a potato.
Take in strays. Pay the vet. Say amen.
Wear your silver and turquoise to knead tortilla dough.

Look the clerk in the eye over food stamps, as though
survival and revenge are close friends.
Four roads to payday: beans and rice, flour, Crisco.

Weed the garden when angry; kneel in each long row.
Zucchini's one thing you don't have to defend.
Wear your silver and turquoise to knead tortilla dough.

Drop everything and pick when the blackberries glow.
Write letters of protest. Root for underdogs. Like *alone*.
Four ways to payday: beans and rice, flour and Crisco.

Bring your mother home to die so your daughter knows
love is stronger than what cannot be forgiven.
Wear your silver and turquoise to knead tortilla dough.
Four paths to payday: beans and rice, flour, Crisco.

Advice from La Llorona

—a found poem

Each grief has its unique side.
Choose the one that appeals to you.
Go gently.
Your body needs energy to repair the amputation.
Humor phantom pain.

Your brain cells are soaked with salt;
connections fail unexpectedly and often.
Ask for help.
Accept help.

Read your grief like the daily newspaper:
headlines may have information you need.
Scream. Drop-kick the garbage can across the street.

Don't feel guilty if you have a good time.
Don't act as if you haven't been hit by a Mack Truck.
Do things a little differently
but don't make a lot of changes.
Revel in contradiction.

Talk to the person who died.
Give her a piece of your mind.

Try to touch someone at least once a day.
Approach grief with determination.
Pretend the finish line doesn't keep receding.
Lean into the pain.
You can't outrun it.

First Step

I take a cotton sack
of tobacco
to the women's drum,
ask for an honor dance.
I wrap a strand
of your turquoise
around the bag,
tuck a twenty
under the beads.
Andrew Jackson
is good for something,
you'd say.
The women confer, sweat-streaked
in San Juan Bautista's heat.
They decide they have the right song.

My daughter dances
beside me, her first time.
Two young cousins
you never met
step behind us, and
my half-sisters
who loved your beauty
and remember your kindness
add their footsteps
to the drum
and the woman warrior's song.

Tobacco killed you.
Tobacco honors you.
There has to be a balance
somewhere—
somewhere, a lesson.

Are you teaching me,
or am I
teaching you?

Medicine
is powerful.
What cures,
also kill. What kills
draws us into a circle.
Maybe our feet stitch
this wound closed
one dusty step
at a time,
create a scar;
outline
the first healing skin.

Part Two: *Drowning*

Drowning

Cold eats my skin
bites muscle, sucks marrow.
Oblivion oozes down my throat
into hidden brachial tubes.
A sudden rock, granite hard,
slices through my veins.
I enter a giant fish
deep in her sandy cave, slip
right through her silver sharp scales,
lodge in her gut:
grandmother of all fish
eggs spilt tight and shiny
among the pebble-children
of mountains. She cradles me,
sings of moss, stone, silt, mud;
she rolls her round fish eyes
that never blink
she says *swim!*
spits me out
between needle-thin teeth.
I panic at the surface:
clutch a clumsy, ragged breath
of thanks.

Tongues

My daughter can't speak. I ask her to open her mouth. She reveals a small, sharp piece of white paper embedded in the side of her tongue. When I begin to pull it out, her tongue splits open all along the length; as I pull, an entire piece of paper emerges. I expect her to scream with pain, but she doesn't. I pull and pull. At the back of her tongue, the paper has grown into her muscle. I must reach in with two hands and rip the flesh of her tongue away from the paper. Still, it doesn't hurt. When I have removed the paper, I stand back, wordless, breathless. My daughter and I look at one another. Her mouth is still slightly open; the separation of her tongue is clear. It is laid open like a sole, like a fillet. I cannot imagine how she will manage to speak. I cannot imagine what language she will need to learn, or already knows.

Duende

The Duende loves ledges and wounds . . .
— LORCA

You make the birds come out in a storm—
sleek seagulls, flagrant pigeons, weathered crows,
the small arrow-like swallows—they want
the air, an immoderate sweetheart whose lovemaking
flings inhibitions into wind's laughing face.

You are that divine despair the suicide knows:
the skeleton of Abandon dancing with plump Grace,
Hedonism gently lifting her skirts to flirt with Sanctity:
Duende! The trees are empty of leaves and song.
You seize these poor creatures, lift and dump and swirl
their bodies almost past limits of feather and hollow bone.
Wings open, beaks sharp, they ride the thrust of unseen
currents till their cries are lost in journey, or abduction.

The beaten sky is flushed with rain.
Duende, you push our souls across a consecrated line.

Echolocation

—for the bats at Point Defiance Zoo

All day long you flutter through artificial night;
hover, sway, wrap furred bodies in leathery shawls
after aborted flight, cling to false stalactites.
Do you know when the moon outside is full,
do you miss the veering, all-out beats
of easy strength across the lunar face,
every stroke of wingspan a simple masterpiece?
Do you remember the soaring, twirling, swooping pace,
the snap of insects' chitinous shells,
soft velvet of a moth's frantic wings?
You eat, excrete, mate, bear young in your tiny cell
but does a warm summer night's calling
echo like a long jagged cave twisting deep into stone,
reverberate against your blood and bone?

La Llorona's Daughter

I'm wearing a red cowboy hat with white lacing around the edge of the brim, a black vest and chaps with white cow skulls, cowboys on horses, and bulls painted all over. Both hands grip the saddlehorn. The pony is dressed up, too: a black bridle studded with faux silver studs, a strap that comes around his neck and meets at a little shield over his chest. My feet dangle above fancy stirrups. The pony even has saddlebags, though they are flat as pancakes. It is a generous detail. The pony's eye is unnerving. It's sheer white. I think he's blind. His head hangs in captive boredom, both ears back. Is he listening to me laugh, or whine? My black hair is cut short, just below my ears, and brushed to the right like a boy's, revealing a widow's peak. There's even a red bandana knotted around my neck, the ends flying out over my left shoulder. At this age, in these clothes, it's hard to tell I'm a girl. The bit is pulled hard in the pony's mouth, and he bares his teeth a little. I must have just gotten home from kindergarten. I must be five. I remember walking across the cement overpass, coming home to my mother. I remember living in these apartments—the pale stucco that would rip my skin when I slammed up against it, hot afternoons playing under the big yucca. But I wasn't five then—I was only 2, 3. By kindergarten I'd already been lost and redeemed, like a sweater left behind on a bus; my father had disappeared, leaving behind only the god-like scent of *Tres Flores*. I didn't know where he was, or that it would be over a decade before I saw him again. By kindergarten, we'd moved into the little house with Tom. So where/when is this photograph? There are parts of my life I can't remember. There are parts of my life I'm not sure ever happened. Maybe I had a twin brother no one told me about; maybe that's him on the pony, grinning, dimpled, an Indian vaquero with a reckless and ready glint in his raven black eyes. Black and white pony, black and white chaps and vest, red hat and bandana, black and brown child. I wonder what his name was. Juan. Carlito. Maybe Innocencio. Maybe he rode off on that pony, crossed the overpass into the barren range beyond. Maybe he'll look me up some day, an Indian Peter Pan who's never aged, say, *hey, you know that kid on the pony? That's me.* And I'll know where the other half of me went.

Sleeping Beauty, 1978

He kisses me and I fall asleep for twenty years,
transported to a happier world. In this dream we move
to the East Coast, following his ex-wife and two young sons.
Boston is all light and color, jewel
of New England. Maples spew red, orange, scarlet
froth like leafy fountains down Commonwealth Ave,
ignite old brick on Marlborough Street, stream unchecked
into the planned chaos of Olmstead's Fenway.
October mornings, the Green Line disgorges car after car
of professors, teachers, college students bound
for a hundred schools, all stone and ivy,
slanted sidewalks awash in ankle-deep fire
that whispers *textbooks, wool sweaters, hot chocolate.*
I walk the Riverway invisible as a ghost,
believe in heroes and damsels in distress, hope
without disappointment, Sunday nights studying
till dawn because weekends are for the pumpkin fields
and choosing thick-shelled giants, my hands
guiding the knife for small fists, my heart pounding
against the stubborn walls of stepson forts. I am three thousand
miles from where October means rain, gray sky: home.
I am three thousand miles from where home means
the fury of fathers beating children with belts,
mothers who leave, little brothers whose dear hearts
are twisted into something unspeakable and rank.
I will sleep on for twenty years, until the suck of an infant
at my breast allows me to mother myself,
and the tender mouth of a woman's lips on mine
seeps like a spring into old crevices, leads moisture
to the dormant seed of my own honest heart.

Chianti

Dreams creep along the rocky caverns of my night.
Long sleek tentacles prod empty husks, flow into each crevice

and abyss, extract sweet meat from a small, shelled fantasy.
They like transgressive ones best, taboo spirals of denial.

Dreams spew out inky surprise when interrupted by rude
lights or the slow echo of bedrock cracking 40 years ago.

Other dreams change color when pursued, flash red, indigo,
at last a ghostly green, eluding leviathans of the past.

The slyest dreams don't stalk but stroke the wet skin of my legs,
bend my naked bones like a contortionist's flight of fancy.

My dreams roam unbridled in the blasphemous depths
of one a.m., babble in a world with no language, no alphabet.

The truth I knew before birth luring me back again,
down again. It breaks my heart to surface for a breath of air.

The Twin Sister Your Mother Never Mentioned

When you lie on your bed at twilight
before the autumn equinox
and the moon burns white on your wrists,
cuts across your cheek, she curls
into you, fits her head along the crook
of your arm, her warm back to your breasts
hips to your thighs—
restless as a child who can't sleep.

She accompanies you like a ghost
who haunts the same house for one hundred years
hoping someone will come back.
In shadows, you glimpse
her scarred brown arm, pale palm
lying open on a faded blue and white quilt.

When you rise to answer your daughter's cry,
this woman walks beside you
shoulder to shoulder, like someone
you should know—
spirit of a woman
you will meet one hundred years from now.

The Place Where Grief and Rage Live

It's big, that space.
Measure it in years
instead of inches—
four decades high,
one memory wide,
five centuries deep.
Multiply by
time lost to find
the total area.
Grief and Rage
live down there
as punishment;
troublesome children
sent to their room
and forgotten.

Denied daylight,
Grief and Rage cry,
fight, grow sharp-
toothed and mean
inside pale hairless
skin. Their eyes
glisten with madness;
that's how they stay sane
enough to stay
alive. What do we do

when someone
slips them a pick,
or they jimmie the lock,
or craft their own key
from leftover debris
and emerge,
escape, get free?

How do we tell
our loved ones,
warn of the violence
Rage might commit
when laughed at?
What if there's no room

for Grief's wails of anguish,
the painful, slow stories?
Putting them back
isn't easy,
but you can do it: lure
with the promise
of a sweet, a drug.
Threats of ridicule
work, too, bribes,
brainwashing,
blackmail. Get them back
into that place
where Grief and
Rage live, slam
the door, lock it hard,
walk away.

Grief and Rage live in the lining
of your womb,
clotted walls
of your artery,
unleashed cells growing
into your children's lungs—
you won't know
where it is
until it's too late
to rehabilitate,

too late to execute,
too late for anything
except Regret.

She lives
anywhere she wants.

Husband

You come to me in our daughter's room
as I change her sheets from puppies to clowns.
We rest a minute in the spring light,
arms around each other's mysterious bodies.
I wonder if this counts: how you've loved me,

how I tried to love you. When it's over, after
more hurt than you deserve, it's only one moment
out of half a lifetime. Will we know a new capacity
for pain? When our marriage is over, longer
than I deserve, remember I cried as if a world were ending,

remember this ruptured moment when something
unbidden and passionate emerged from my body
as if we gave birth one last time together.
Can we heal, is this strange labor a cure?
My desire demands a life of its own, sucks air,

gives tongue to words you swear you can't hear.
You disguise the birth-cry as a curse, a flaw, a mistake.
brought on by warm spring rain. I'll try to live your lie
but this creature shares our house now; raw, hungry
at my breast, and my milk coming in like a storm.

10%

It is all you'll ever see.

The rest lies floating
beneath the surface
in cold blue light,
radiant.

Only the creatures of ice
know my jagged edges
broken by weight—
smooth curves worn

against the shoulders of ancient currents.
Seals diving for sustenance,
white bears hunting

fat seals. Whales, singing
as they feast
on the rich fields

of tiny beings
flowing ceaselessly
around my immense,
hidden body.

Tonight you were full
of bravado, full of beer.
He knows, I thought,

and for a moment
was exposed.
I could spill
everything

who I loved
who I feared
how it hurt me
what I dream.

I looked back at you,
let my face open,
but all you saw
was a small raw sliver

the indigo halo
of what never thaws.

Driving Past Suicide for Three Novembers

Who will explain it to my children—
this beast called bereftness,
the sharp pre-solstice moon battered by clouds?
Driving home late, too much wine in me,
I know my mother came this way once;
her hands white on the steering wheel, her lips
a tight chrysalis of fear as she drives on
into a void whose end
she can't see, can't hope to find.

Who will tell my children
about their seal-like movements within my belly,
the way my daughter hiccuped inside
till I rocked her back to watery sleep,
how my son's head moved slowly under my ribs
like a large planet crossing
a small universe?

When I arrive home tonight
my husband will reach for me in the dark—
his need, his comfort, his right.
Who will tell my children
marriage is more
than a glistening soul
served up on a silver platter?

Separation

How is it possible for anything to be this still? It's as if all the trees I've listened to in past days pull up short, mute themselves, listen instead for intruders in their midst. No leaves stir, no needles brush against other needles. I know the trees breathe the long continuous unbroken exhale of night, but now they are secretive, wary, voiceless.

"Four or five?" someone asks, out of the blackness, "Four, or five?" her voices rises with urgency, a deadline she knows and I don't. Another woman's voice seems to answer her: "I don't have time." But that's no answer. Is it?

Downstairs, out of the neighbor's open window, radio music erupts, a rock song with guitars, drums, vocals screaming, ". . . a beautiful day!"—plays for a full minute until he awakens, finds the off switch, hits, misses, hits. As if the world has had its wake-up call, a woman appears at the end of the block. Her head is wrapped in a scarf, and above the tinkling of her dog's tags she speaks one soft word, or clears her throat. After she crosses the intersection in front of my high porch, a white truck pulls through. Another dog barks furiously five blocks away; a back-up beeper sounds to the southeast.

The fingers of my right hand, gripping a pen, grow numb. I pause to flex them, pump blood to the extremities. The tips tingle. A nerve is compressed somewhere. I've grown monstrous to survive a marriage that threatens to devour me. Will I grow uglier still, turn to lead with the guilt of saving myself?

Ex

I want someone to save you. For example, your old professor, who taught you to love history, played basketball like a pro; once, he was your measure of scholarship and sportsmanship, mind and body in control. At the faculty meeting he sits up high in the back row, dressed in his Hush Puppies, brown slacks, coat and tie. He listens to debate leaning forward, gray head bowed, hands wrapped around his long furled umbrella. Does the lack of progress frustrate or bore him? I want to walk up the gray-green carpeted steps, move between the rows of lecture hall seats, see him raise his head at my approach. I want to ask if he remembers you— Your fascination with Huxley, Europe, politics at home. Does he remember your blown-out knee, the shy blonde girl in your second year (the wife before me), the younger brother who shone on the court instead of you? I want to say to him, that boy is 56 years old now. Twice divorced. Four children. He teaches high school. Tell me, professor—do you remember him? Can you save him? I tried.

I want someone to save your soul. Maybe an old friend from your small hometown, a boy who used to ride his bike down the alley to ask, "Wanna shoot hoops?" and was awkward, good-natured despite your smooth jumpshot, your quick rebounds, your youth. His father gambled away the family house once. By the time I meet him by accident at a conference for Queers and their allies, your buddy's beard is silver, shot with red, much like yours. He tells me, "The day my daughter came out to me as a lesbian was the day I knew a moment of pure grace." He describes your house on Sixth Street, your sisters, your love of the game. He never mentions his father. These days he travels from conference to church to counseling session, spreading the word of his daughter's revelation. I ask him for his phone number, email, his card. I want him to call you. I want him to offer you his warm sweatered shoulder, want him to save you from the bitter knives unraveling your proud soul. I want someone to save you. I can't.

The Language of Prophets

Out of grey clouds
right to left
one hawk
eight herons over
dark water.
One fierce year—
eight years of stillness.
Green pines take
what fog lets go.

Heron

You were like a song to me—
I dreamt those words last night,
held onto them all the way to waking,
waited all day to write. But it's evening now,
I can't recall what came next, or what I was thinking
when you came to me, Heron, let out a wrought-iron
rasp; your blue and silver cape, ribboned crest flying
and yet without a song
                                        —but my ears thrum with it,
cruel, tattered grace, rough edges like notes cut bare,
less gifted, more generous than any songbird—
that was it: *you were like a song to me—*
you, my heart, my memory,
my lost one come back: you,
my voice, my own voice.

Part Three: *A Trick of Grace*

A Trick of Grace

> There are women in Africa who can walk
> further, carry more, and arrive at their
> destination better rested than army recruits or
> longshoremen bearing similar loads. Researchers
> say the women move like pendulums.

I move toward you
as if I know how to carry
this thing in my heart,
as if my body can bear
desire and trust, want and faith.

Some days I stagger
like a raw recruit, sweating
under an awkward pack;
some days I blush with shame
like the longshoreman
who can't hoist one more pound.

But I'll learn this honest walk—
how to sway, wait, balance.
The secret lies in letting
what has the power to crush
pull me forward, instead.

I move toward you,
though it takes years.
I relish this weight,
what my body cradles:
transformation
in all her intimate aspects.
O, I want to be graceful for you!
I want to arrive
at my destination

bearing this gift,
breathless only
from the sight
of your face.

Arrow Song

I am the arrow shot into morning.
I am the obsidian tooth. I bite wind, cloud, sky.
I leave no trail behind me—
just the hum of wood and feather.
I do not heed high stone mountains,
the wide wrinkled land, cobalt rivers.
I am the arrow of purpose and intent.
I eat a thousand miles for breakfast,
cold altitude for lunch; I find my supper
at journey's end when I lodge suddenly
against your breast. Your heart opens
like a Cimmerian red wine, or summer twilight.
You take me in, still quivering with flight.
Your skin heals tenderly over shaft, quill,
my glassy raven edges. I am the arrow
who flies so true my kiss leaves only
a small clean scar. Touch it now
for remembrance, for honor.

From a Dream, I Wake to Tender Music

From a dream, I wake to tender music.
You sit nearby—my boy. Your lips
hover over your instrument, fine fingertips
press and rise lightly along mellow wood grain,
round openings of the flute's body. Your song
doesn't falter till I slide to the floor,
kneel before you. I touch turquoise sleeves,
rolled back; place my trembling fingers
over your wrist where an old,
familiar blood runs hard. Our mouths open.
Our kiss makes no sound, but outside
the river leaps, a long wild note.
I find a cry like all the rivers we've lost:
waters captured, dammed, living still.

Love Poem to a Butch Woman

This is how it is with me:
so strong, I want to draw the egg
from your womb and nourish it in my own.
I want to mother your child made only
of us, of me, you; no borrowed seed
from any man. I want to re-fashion
the matrix of creation, make a human being
from the human love that passes between
our bodies. Sweetheart, this is how it is:
when you emerge from the bedroom
in a clean cotton shirt, sleeves pushed back
over forearms, scented with cologne
from an amber bottle—I want to open
my heart, the brightest aching slit
of my soul, receive your pearl.
I watch your hands, wait for the sign
that means you'll touch me,
open me, fill me; wait for that moment
when your desire leaps inside me.

Mesa Verde

The earth is salmon-colored here, cracked
into plates like the shell of a giant turtle.
It is a place I've seen in a dream.
Our faces tingle with the heat of sun,
the fiery way we look at one another.
When we drive down the steep road
back to the highway, you stop
the car so I can gather a stalk of some
rosy blossom, unknown, unidentified.
Your hands gently cup the waxy petals,
fingertips outlining leaves as if you know
how to stroke color and scent, coax forth
a name like a blood secret. The aroma
of honey, nectar, hangs in dry air.
Tiny gold ants crawl on the hairy stem,
seek the deep center, enter it.
As we drive on, I leave the branch behind.
The ants will find their way home carrying
a burden so sweet it needs no name,
a story to tell about being taken up,
removed, finding the intricate paths back.

Music Like Red Earth

We drive north against evening's
soft purple. The sun sets for a long time;
we are heading into the solstice.
It is that part of the land
where people carve farms
in the shadow of mesas and sandstone
temples. When metal scratches her,
earth rises up thick and red as old blood.

On this thin ridge of road we roll down
the windows. The steering wheel burns
my hands; my hair comes unbraided,
flies into the wind. You ask me
not to bind it up again. Smiling
beside me, you play a cherry red flute
at 65 miles per hour: rich waltzes,
fast French tunes, sad Portuguese ballads
and the pitiful sailor's shanty
that makes us laugh. You name the melodies

that slope between one low hill
and the next. Along the ditch, tall grasses
sway with silky tops lit scarlet and hot.
Our passing makes them leap like celebrants
rooted in one place but dancing
with all their hearts nonetheless.
Notes and chords rush into the car
like a lost flock of wild birds;
tangle in our hair, stream out, soothed,
into slow twilight.
In the morning we will breathe
their feathery scent on our pillows.
Tonight, you play music like red earth,
honor what we have found here
the best you can: with the stain

of a sacred color and that rich red
flute singing, breathing,
for both of us.

First Time

Remember the mandolin Leigh brought out
of an upstairs closet, that night we stopped
for dinner? She offered the instrument to you:
sleek gleaming wood, sonorous tone.
You bent your head to capture the notes
of a song you hadn't thought of in years.
While you played I watched Leigh's face.
She stood quietly in a shadow between
the lamp and her husband. Her long hair
rippled like ink against the wall's smooth line.
She was remembering something beautiful.
You remembered it, too. You entered
the mandolin's voice the way you would enter me
later that night for the first time.

Steele Street

Under the red-fury glare of my husband
and the heated jealous eyes of my children,
you and I stood beside your car, our faces
flushed with raw, half-crazy hunger.
You held me against your body, whispered
into my hair, "I love you." We stood in the street,
surrounded by the geography of my life.
The old working class houses, cut or uncut grass,
salmon-pink roses unpruned. Under our feet, cracked
asphalt and old brick, dirt and sewers,
layers of civilization's debris.
The city's archeology, muffled histories
of a relocated tribe. Commencement Bay glittered
like steel. Tahoma loomed huge on the horizon,
an angry exiled god.

Back inside, I could not feel my limbs,
my mouth, my lungs.
Everything was stone. My children
approached me, asked questions,
went away. You were driving fast,
your fingers gripping
the hot steering wheel, your dear face
stern, twisted by the labor
of leaving. I could hear you
whispering my name.
You did not come back.
You were not going to come back.

I broke like the sheer face
of a cliff, like crystal
inherited from the family matriarch,
like a carapace:
every bone in my body,
each cell. I broke and I broke

as if each crack
were a catalyst,
as if my soul were made of dominos,
as if breaking
were a secret disease hidden
in my genes,
triggered by your touch. I broke
for hours, for days,
for years—flailing, snatching
at fragments and shards,
sure that healing mean setting
each break, believing
what's shattered
should be made whole.

> I wish I'd known then:
> we must break the casting
> to reveal what's been fired within.

A Ceremony for Giving You Up

I wrap strands of your hair into a band around my finger, twist ends tight until the circle loses any beginning or end. I stroke my cheek with a smooth piece of sandstone found on a path winding high above the Uinta forest, taste how layers of time separate. I bury my face in the sheets you slept in; the moan I cannot contain lingers in cotton fibers. I carry the fading scent of your desire in my arms like a dead child, immerse longing in water. It is a ceremony like dawn, a ritual of new prayers and sacrifices: tobacco, coffee, red wine. Each day is a ceremony no one sees, a ceremony I must perform again and again, until I believe it. I know it is a ceremony of power: my heart rings open at every step on the altar of your name.

Clean

Alone in the shower this morning,
I remember the white cloth
on my breast, the vivid cinnamon of your hand
slowly stroking, cupping.
I remember the shame in my body,
creases of childbearing on my
belly and thighs, shadows of abuse against
my throat. I remember thinking my scars
were something to hide. I remember knowing
all this, still asking for your touch
everywhere.

You knelt to soap my calves
and feet, light musician's fingers following the lines
of my spine, shoulders. You rose
before me, water streaming over
our smooth bodies.
I took the cloth from your hand
and bathed you, sweetheart,
in beauty.

Shopping

means not being able to walk past the men's clothing department without seeing a shirt your former lover would have looked beautiful wearing, or a silk tie that, at one time, you would have bought her as a love gift for her to wear one afternoon, the fine material like wet fire against your breasts. Tailored slacks, in the brand she liked to wear best, call to your hand, and though you quickly turn your head and walk on, your fingertips sting for the darts at the waist, or the sharp teeth of the zipper beneath a trim cotton edge. You don't, ever, enter the men's undergarment section, though sometimes the store displays boxers in unexpected places. You know the construction by heart, how the panel slides aside, or the tiny pearlescent buttons—

But you are with your children, a daughter near as tall as yourself, who needs her first bra; a younger son who is fine and lanky and agrees to a new pair of jeans. As you walk through department stores, malls, check sizes and colors, you are torn, halved. One part mother, fulfilled by the squeeze of your children's hands. One part lover, aching, wet, as if it were only this morning that you reached over in the car as she drove and stroked her face, lips. You remember the crisp cream-colored collar of her shirt that day, unbuttoning it at the neck, the fine crisp strands of hair at her throat. And she opened her mouth, took your fingers lightly between her teeth, sucked so gently that you cried out her name in warning. She took possession of your hand, hesitated only a split second, drew your fingers down between her legs, pressed them hard against the zipper. The fabric's weave was tattooed into your palm.

"I'll dress for you," she whispered. But she dresses for another woman, the lover she went back to. In her top drawer, in the back, beneath rolls of black socks, boxers, T-shirts, wrapped in silk, she keeps your picture. You wonder—days like this, you wonder—why your image doesn't just go up in flames.

Old Territory. New Maps.

You plan an uncomplicated path
through Colorado's red dust,
around the caustic edge of Utah's salt flats
a single night at a hotel
in the Idaho panhandle. Our plans change.
It's spring, we are two Indian women alone
together and the days open:
sunrise on a fine long road,
antelope against dry hills,
heron emerging from dim fields.
You tell me this is a journey
you've always wanted to take.
You ask me to tell you what I want.

I want my longing to miraculously
bring you through the barrier of your skin
into my blood so that I can possess you
entirely and yet be entirely possessed.
You say no, your face tight with pain, tears
burning your eyes, hands clenching the steering wheel.
I believe you. We drive hundreds of miles
across deserts sculpted by wind and story,
and I learn the distance from my hand to your thigh,
your mouth to my mouth, the curve of a collar
along a warm, smooth neck.
You grin as if no one has ever seen you thus:
naked, savage, happy.
That is the beginning of yes.

Ghosts are everywhere.
We hear them singing on that mountain in Ute country,
the cries of your flute pleasuring old spirits.
Like those people whose land we cross,
we don't live by lines drawn on paper.
Instead, we mark the waterfall of shy kisses,

a dry windy town where we exchange secrets in whispers,
the high cliff hollow that shelters us
on the edge of the Uinta forest.
Wildflowers bend beneath our bodies,
cup the trembling weight of touch.
We wander for awhile in a place vast enough
to contain all possibilities.

After twelve hundred miles together
we enter green forest thick along a fearless river.
This dense topography we can't see through,
can't find the horizon to judge distances
or the arc of the sun to know east from west.
There at last you clasp my hand, guide it
to a place beyond maps,
no universe I have ever known.
It is a raw landscape; we are the sojourners
overcome by the perilous shock of arrival.
We stop the car, walk by the river,
clumsy, frightened by desire. I wish
for more than body or soul can bear.

Sweet, these are the maps we made together,
territories we foolishly vowed to own.
Here, the place we wandered off the map,
moved deep into a land without scars
where every direction took us home
but no place could give us shelter.
I don't know how to survive awakening
in a woman's body with a child's
broken heart. I fall on my knees, our love
a bare stone on the windowsill between us.
How can I learn this trick, will your body
back to the other side of my skin? Help me
translate loss the way this land does—

flood, earthquake, landslide—
terrible, and alive.

Dawn

No one's fated or doomed to love anyone.
The accidents happen, we're not heroines,
they happen in our lives like car crashes
books that change us, neighborhoods
we move into and come to love.
— ADRIENNE RICH, Love Poem XVII

∼

Trees in my neighborhood dance in quiet wee hours. Cedars take turns waiting for the wind to come, lift their limbs in green ceremony. The oaks still have their leaves, pines drop dry cones onto the wet earth. Each species moves in her own favorite sway. I listen and watch, eyelids made heavy, heart blessedly silent.

∼

I left the marriage house with almost no belongings, re-possessed myself from yard sales, thrift stores, the generosity of friends. Now, towels or silverware match only by chance. Inside myself is an entire houseful of furnishings. All the dreams, actions, words I've kept locked up in the attic of my soul.

∼

My mother, whose name means *dove*, tells me Indian languages originate from the gleaming throats of birds. A friend whose father is mentally ill won't do the automatic writing that feeds her art; the gush of it frightens her. She thinks her own words can lock her up.

∼

The sun rises, breaches heavy clouds. We call this sapphire light *dawn*, but what do we know? Where is the foggy edge between then and *now*? Maybe it is the difference between inner and outer worlds.

I try to leave the old grief of my gut behind. Make it only a dream, an accident. Make her not leave me this time.

~

Surprise me with Shoshone Falls. Direct me, *turn left here*, say *Let's take this exit*. The road is suddenly a crevasse: opens jagged in this flat earth, slants fast down to the river. A gift. You saved this moment to please me. The Indian girl at the gate takes our user fee and grins as if you'd called ahead to conspire. *I'm bringing a woman to the Falls this afternoon*, you might have confided. *Make sure they roar real good*. The waters are wide as my hopes. Out on the boat dock, our bare feet in cold current, you kiss me: lips pursed, trembling, shy for all your boasts. It's what I want, though. Innocence; the almost virginal state before passion. The love of children who plan to marry each other when they've grown up. Later we can teach each other about desire. Today I want Shoshone Falls, our brown feet in frothy waters, even the blue truck of good old boys who back their boat-trailer down to the ramp, interrupt us, cause us to stand up and move on.

~

If there is a time of day when I can forgive myself, it is almost, barely, not quite dawn.

~

Robins and house sparrows flit between the indistinct lines of houses, between what is dormant, what awakens.

~

Forgiveness imagines us as shadowy dreams.

～

Just before the smallest cry of sun is a crack where peace hides. If I am quick, sometimes we glimpse one another from afar. Your eyes are wide, more fathomless than I remember.

Burning the Baskets

The first coil of our meeting a flower turning
toward mistake Yellow outline of antelope See?
your gaze Burning the Baskets Bright paths of
our words as they fork toward to Navajo Lake
Sleek maidenhair fern Harsh zigzags of
yes/no/yes/no! yes beargrass like river's breath
Dusty road Sleek leaves lit by emerald blood a
prayer to cleanse We came of a kiss flood of
yellow butterflies Beneath strands We cannot
break stitches we never spliced our design
complete our story our hearts beat together
charms to bind you I've clung flying to these
baskets shaped my life's work ai'ai ai I was
wrong a stillborn pattern Baskets of paper
baskets of impossible design fill with grief
wail back into this world wail back into my skin
the one who dying

Burning the Baskets

The first coil of our meeting I am a flower turning toward the warmth of your gaze See? our words bright paths forking toward mistake past yellow outlines of antelope the dusty road to Navajo Lake sleek maidenhair fern Harsh zigzags of [yes/no/yes/no] . Yes. Beargrass like river's breath beneath leaves lit by emerald blood a prayer to bless the comet of a kiss a flood of yellow butterflies flying strands we cannot break stitches we cannot complete my life's work. I've clung to these baskets shaped our story spliced charms to bind you was wrong a stillborn pattern our hearts never beat together. ai, ai ai baskets of paper baskets of impossible design baskets of living full of grief bumback bumback into my skin back into the sacred embered this world entered the searing being

[82]

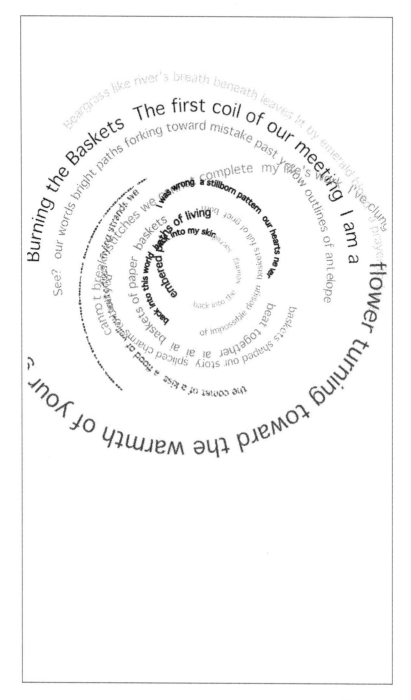

Burning the Baskets

The first coil of our meeting I am a flower turning toward the warmth of your

Beargrass like river's breath beneath leaves lit by emerald light clump

our words bright paths forking toward mistake past yourself's window outlines of antelope

See? our words ... Cannot be broken strands we ... stitches we ... I was wrong complete my ... a stillborn pattern our hearts ne...

baskets of paper baskets paths of living into my skin

back into this world endured

of impossible design

beat together al al al baskets shaped our story spliced charms

the comet of a kiss a flood of

Part Four: *Dar a Luz*

Dar a Luz
"Giving Birth"; literally, "to give to the light"

La Llorona gives birth on Wednesday
shortly after ten-thirty a.m.,
crouches over the scarred, sticky
maplewood floor
in a studio apartment
just off an alley behind the liquor store.

She pants patiently
through her sweat,
pulls the pulsing, slick
infant close to her empty breasts.
The baby takes a dry nipple,
suckles hard.
La Llorona leans back
against the mildewed wall.
The tune she hums hangs like a whip
in the yellow air: *Bone of my bone,*
flesh of my flesh. You shall be called . . .
Into the blossoming chrysalis
of her child's ear, La Llorona whispers a name
to keep the story spinning
despite
the desolate, ugly
detours we take
away from
emergence:

Lovely, Exquisite,
Gorgeous, Splendid,
Magnificent,
Mountain,
Dawn,
Deer

Portrait of the Beloved as a Young Lifeguard

You perch
gawky as a heron
at the top of steel stilts;

legs brown from obligations
in the sun. You witness for the water.
The sky hangs heavy as white steel.

This is killer heat, the kind that drives
us into anything wet: waders,
wallowers, paddlers alike.

Mothers gasp along shallows
in swimsuits they've stopped
trying to camouflage. Young girls flirt, slicked up

with lotion and lust—
is it a pool? the Atlantic?
a local lake? You're on duty:

long hair pulled back out of the way,
sunglasses hiding your eyes, mouth open
as if to breathe for them all. You anticipate

the foolish one sucked into riptide,
recognize the arc and lurch of another's leg cramps,
monitor the one who always swims out

too far. Gallantry disguised as a girl,
you will rescue every drowning woman
whose head sinks below

the lukewarm, deceptive waters,
whose limbs go limp in despair,
whose ragged ripples pull you from your post,

signal *save me save me save me.*

Smoke

I.

It's your one vice, you're gonna give it up
some day; you, in your white T-shirt, sleeves rolled,
a pair of old Levi's and scuffed running shoes.
You lean against your dusty truck,
squint half-assed guilt into the sunrise.
You nod as I pass; we acknowledge the craving
that pulls us out of bed, seeks air, river,
the grace of wet firs. My skin tingles as I cross
the river's rapids toward—I can't say it aloud,
don't dare—the love of a woman? You watch
me walk, ache, breathe. You take note of the flush
on my face, raise a cocky eyebrow. You don't know me
well enough to say, *take care*. And what if you did?
That truck, those shoes, make promises you want to keep.

II.

At dusk, your cigarette glows heated orange.
I blush coming back from my lover's arms;
can you see every kiss on my skin, the marks
of her mouth incandescent tattoos? All week
you watch me, the scent of your tobacco drifting
like an offering across evening's soft green.
Once, mid-day, you smoke after lunch as my lover
and I stow laundry in her car—an excuse
to be away, and alone—you smile: "Laundry?"
I can't meet your eyes. In the car, my lover grins
at me, "Do you think she suspects?"
She takes my hand firmly in hers, brings it
to her lips; my mouth fills with fresh desire.
I know you'll never tell.

III.

You write, . . . *six weeks into a stop-smoking campaign—*
sure sign of new love! your heart hopes
for something beautiful on the other side
of the river—but your sparse letters arrive thin
and frayed by some force I can't see, as if sent
from the front lines of one undeclared war
to another. I throw words back over the moat,
beseiged in my own house. Ah, can *I* quit?
Children stir down the hallway like sweet dreams
rattled loose in the night; their father drinks strong coffee
downstairs, alone. It's time we grew up, I agree.
We wake in warm beds instead of cold
parking lots, and call this progress. It's a lie.
We love 'normal' more than we love ourselves.

IV.

You still wear those jeans, but swear you never
rolled cigarettes up in a t-shirt sleeve. Funny
how my memory invented things that didn't happen.
We walk across the bridge together; lay our tattered souls
to burn like sage, dry and pungent. Same trees, same rain,
but our nights are new as skin. My palms astonish me,
recall the smooth plain of your back, luminous pearls
of your sweat as you moved through the riddle of me,
sharing a cedar-sweet bed and the full moon's impish
glance between shades. I should've known you'd revel
in details, paint my breasts with your long fine hair,
spilling sleek, fleet lines of blackbirds there,
a tenderness of scars. What we've erased in passion,
we compose now in the blue smoke, black ash of thanks.

My Moon

The moon, luminous egg, tells me
my womb is starry,
knows light from eons ago
when I swam into the constellations
of my mother's body even as, quickening,
she lodged within her own mother's flesh.

We name moon's aspects like children
we might conceive, sweet sounds
called at night across distance:
blue moon for what is rare, *harvest moon*
for what is ready, *green corn moon*
for the tassled ears, sweet kernels of milky youth.
What name does moon give us?
Her body loves us so, dancing
through us, around us,
waking tides of salty blood, water,
the soft tissue just beneath luminous skin.
Surely she calls out some word in her own lunar language,
brings us closer to her face in longing
if not in bone. There's song in the stars,
though perhaps we've heard it too much,
can no longer decipher constance.

This August evening I drive north,
midwife to unexpected death as I bleed.
Moon follows me along the silvery slough,
plows tulip fields, breaks edges of volcanic islands
shaped by fire. I've carried my own unborn grandchildren
already, urged desire and grief toward union
in the breath of a lover. It's a long turn toward brilliance,
toward birth of the life our desire creates.
May our faces reflect that rising.

Home

You are a hunter of auctions, of chickweed,
skinner of bear and moose, multiplier of mosses,
stitcher of quilts and tattered women's hearts,
creek-wader, walker of clay and smooth granite paths,
digger of red ochre earth, guardian of the cedar grove,
black walnut perfume-maker, watcher of thorn-promise berries,
coltsfoot shoots in the road, deer droppings in meadows, wild
turkey at dawn; you gather redbuds early ahead
of the heat, place tender petals on my tongue before
breakfast. Ah, sweetheart, this pillaged continent's not
what I've lost, not the sanctuary searched for since birth.
All lusts ever harbored, each stolen deed of desire—
these fantasies aren't native land. Where's home?
I can't draw a map, but I've wandered each curve and hollow.
The place that knows me is a woman.

Fencing Out the Deer

Our host apologizes for the men, the chainsaws,
the burning pile of tree branches dropping white ash
on the pages of our open books
but adds, *We work so hard, getting roses to bloom*
in this weather, everything looking great—then
we come out one morning and it's all
gone, trampled, eaten by those damn deer . . .

That afternoon I stand behind you, arms locked
around your fine waist, mouth in your clean hair,
look up: see the men frozen, a crooked tree branch
in each hand, forgetting something crucial
in the distance between fallen tree and bonfire.
Staring. Gently you step out of my arms,
walk casually back into the cabin. I wonder

what they think in the late afternoon,
when poetry's consumed us but our bodies
still hum with the energy of creation.
Do they pause at the cries of my small birth,
do they wonder which place your fingers
have touched, and how? Do they imagine
these are roses not meant for two dark-haired
women, long braids coming undone
in each other's hands?

Sparks at twilight weld wire to steel poles
ten feet high all around the meadow.
When dawn breaks tomorrow, roses can bloom safely,
saved from the velvet glistening noses, supple tongues of deer,
their greedy teeth and sharp feet.

In the evening we lie down, and you trust
that I won't go too far, too fast, take too much.
For the first time you breathe *now, oh—now—*
and sweetheart, I would wait at that fence forever
for this moment when steel parts, invites me in.

Satiate

Satiate: to shimmer like the plumes of a poppy in July, the air around each feathery petal a quiver of fuschia and flagrant; to curve like a tall plant springing up in the cusp of land tended by a possessive woman on one side, voracious deer on the other. *Satiate*: not an end to want, but—given time, or luck, or the right amount of loss—the cry that radiates from a bright paper-lantern seed case, wicks to the wet grass below. *Satiate*: to scoop up a handful, hold it out for your lover to see. She is startled as each ribbony petal undulates, entangled and lively, like strange tongues released from mother language, sent out to search for words of their own—and each tongue chose her.

Shenandoah

Tinier than my smallest fingernail,
kernel of corn, or the size of a
5-year-old's front tooth—
a flaming drop the color of
another dimension—

this strawberry my lover
feeds me tastes like the inside of
an orchid, like June unzipped
blazing its own red stories:

black bears
browsing with elegant carmine
tongues and quarter-moon
canines in a delirium
of discovery,

fine fish roaming like
ruddy Atlantic salmon
through my corpuscles,
faster than osmosis and twice as
glib; denizens of desire
all shine and swagger,

a small seeded heart
beating amidst the leaves
and unruly runners,
waiting
          waiting
                    waiting for redemption
in the shape of a woman's hand.

Ambrosial brute,
ardent fingerling, dearest
kiss of blood,
thank you for the red clay
language, these new names
for hunger.

When I Think of You

your body is the familiar blur
between cabin and garden,
moving from lush seedlings in the basement
to a stainless steel convection oven
where fragrant batches of biscotti
bake firm in your wide clean pans.
In my mind's eye the amber light of logs
washes over your hands;
your quilts hang from the railing
like calendars, each square marking off time.
Are you counting the days of your solitude,
or the years till I come? When I think of you,
I think of silence though it's true
you turn up the news while rinsing sprouts
and talk to the dog as he clatters in and out,
his long black snout homing in on what's forbidden.
Do you tell him things you'd tell me
if I were there right now? Do you ask him
if the snow's still falling, is it piling up
like the weather report predicted? Some things
I can't know and you can't say, even alone
in your house on 72 acres in the saddle between
Little House and Big House Mountains
but sweetheart, there's nothing I want more
than to come in that back door, stomp snow off my boots,
home just ahead of the storm,
hear you tell me
anything.

Leaving Oz

We can't stay in Oz forever, and the drag show
is over, anyway. Dorothy stops us as we cross the threshold,

her wizened charcoal hand on my escort's arm.
"Please, sir," she begins—

you reach for pocket change. Bourbon Street
glitters with the tipsy, the curious, the young;

uninvited company in bedrooms of the homeless.
Dorothy's silver earrings dangle low as southern stars.

She waves your emerald twenty like a flag.
Thank you Jesus! her prayer goes up like fog.

Arm in arm, we walk briskly to our rented hotel room.
We'll wrap up in each other's skin like blankets,

rock each other with the fury of lost and found.
We don't yet have a home together. We can't say,

our bed, our sheets, our pillows. We meet sparingly
in random cities between east and west coasts,

streets that shine like spilled jewels at night, offer us
temporary shelter for a price. Here, there are no rooms

for my children, my son's long-limbed puns,
the smoldering swimming pools of my daughter's eyes;

no winding trails for your shepherd's big feet.
There is no warm basement for your black trays of seedlings,

no office of desk and shelves layered in my poetry
and student's papers; there are no rain barrels stationed

at the corners of the roof, no salamanders nested in the cool
green space beside the foundation. I want you to take me home,

and I want to go home, and those two places are not the same.
Tonight when you undress me, I'll surprise you with black satin.

In this cusp between lives, darling, it's the next best thing
to those ruby red slippers you'd like to see me wear.

Tenderness

I'm filled three times by your hand
and you rest finally against my cheek
your hair all unbraided, water on sand.

You're butch as black leather but supple as sin,
slippery sweetheart all suave and sleek
I measure night's depth by your hand

and fingers teasing like pussywillows on skin;
you'd make stones rise up from the river and speak,
their braided cries streaming like water on sand.

Your tongue smuggles pleasure like contraband
through the mountain pass, beyond the peak—
Yes, I'm clearly getting out of hand

—darling, you must take a firmer stand
with me; remember, we've got this cabin for a week;
how many women have you built by hand?

Words like *sweet baby* aren't typical terms of command
and holding me while I cry isn't quite the technique

I expected; you cradle me, raw, in your hand,
brush back my braids strand by strand.

Highway 126
for Margo

In these days when I am broken
you walk beside me on the highway
between sanity and what I've lost,
guard my left side
on this thin asphalt shoulder
wedged between hulking semi-trucks
and a dry ditch of wildflowers. *Look,* you murmur,
Yellow Evening Primrose swooping right out of rock!
You congratulate clumps of Chamomile clinging
to earth, encourage Black-eyed Susans
staring bright and stark,
caress purple blossoms blazing
like tiny orchids amongst the pebbles.
In the vacant lot knotted with tall stiff grass,
you admire the tumbling
crazed vines and tendrils of wild sweet pea.
Hand on my back, you turn me
into the coolness near the river, onto a carpet
of tiny twin-flowers and lavender stars. You feed me
the hidden too-sweet strawberries I've forgotten,
stoop swiftly to retrieve a feather flashing
indigo and black in the chickweed.
In these days when I am broken,

you find healing herbs and medicines springing up
from dirt and gravel, the cracked ditch wanting rain,
stones churned up by passing cars. *Everything heals,* you say,
even Foxglove cups a secret in its soft paws:
digitalis to ease the racing heart,
or capture it once and for all. We walk
alongside power, or through it—carrying
our illnesses, fearing all giving has gone to grave.
You place crushed stems in my hand,
bathe my fingers in pale green fluids,
tell me *the world is full of cures.*

It will be years and countless walks down other roads
before I see with your eyes:
this land strewn with weeds and miracles
sown in equal number.

Mitzvah

for Margo

This morning my mother's luminous body arcs sharply
up from the bed, her dear olive skin stretched taut groans,
bursting like flames from a throat that can no longer bear
even a trickle of water. I've waited all my life for the woman
she's become: sober, brilliant, proud. I've only had her
for a few years. Here I am, taking care of her again
when I just want to cry in her arms.

I look up, see you on the other side of the bed:
bracing your sturdy shoulders beneath the burden,
easing your arms under my mother's neck, her knees.
Your hips lift in stern grace, weight shifting.
You call her by her name's unshakeable syllables.
You tell her everything's okay. You bathe my mother
so that I can be her daughter for a few minutes longer.

dia de las muertas

It's your own heart, your old heart, buried under the dry brown earth. Buy yourself a handful of sugar skulls, crunch them between your back teeth, make sweet juice of saliva and sugar cane. Let the songs work their seduction; sing yourself hoarse, fake the Spanish words you don't know, will never know. You don't care! One colonizer's tongue is the same as the next. It's yours now—you've earned it, untied it, flayed it, learned how to ride it. Let's dance on this grave, then, in any language so long as they all say goodbye, farewell . . . so long as they all say so long, thanks for all the tears . . . Poor little heart, poor corazoncita, it's all for the best, you just lie there and die, dear one, querida, let in the small beetles, the pink fleshy worms, give up la cuerporita—the worst is over now, you've gone to a better place and we who are left living, we survivors, we dance on your grave, eat empanadas, drink beer, watch bonfires in a daze of relief and excess. Ah, this is the only true revenge: picnicking in the cold November air on the fresh grave of your own worn-out heart. At midnight, your lover plants a new seed in you, a flower only she knows how to coax into bloom. At dawn, she calls down the rain.

Lightning Source UK Ltd.
Milton Keynes UK
UKHW041013241020
372160UK00001B/17